T0288078

Becca Klaver's *Ready for the World* is a daz
witches, and bad princesses, a survival g
With poems created from FB girl party message boards to
Ready for the World is major contemporary while still paying honor to feminist
conceptual art foremothers like Yoko Ono, who taught us the power of words, of
wishes. "A wish is not a luxury," Klaver writes, "They will tell you you can have
no more wishes / And yet we wish well of course we wish." Klaver's spells and
wishes give me permission, give me life.
—Kate Durbin

"A reverse exorcism," *Ready for the World* is on the astrological cusp of Cancer
and carcinogen, analog experience and clickable fantasy. With her selfie timer
set, Becca Klaver takes our hand and skips us through an Insta feed looking-
glass into an introspective grimoire. The girly spectral speakers of the "pink
geometry" mapped in these poems stake their own subjectivity in packs,
through ritual and performativity and raucous laughter. Whether your own
adolescence was blissfully full of besties who Ouija'ed yourselves out of the patri-
archy or not, you can "get that teenage feeling back" with this tricked-out book.
Call in the four elements and stand by for the headrush of magic.
—Arielle Greenberg

Well, right away it's clear that this is about a witch who's trying to reestablish the
connection with nature the lack of which I feel as I'm writing this. Then she joins
the chorus of girls that in a previous time might have hopped around a Christina
Rossetti or Austen churchyard that are now the self-subjects of selfies and visual
autofictions on social media. There's something about the flow of it that reflects
the movements of nature. Maybe that's feminine attraction to digital flow. Yeah,
I said flow… The witch melts and she's reborn in the flow of knowledge. "I am
the motherboard of artifice./ I am, like, too close to nature." Spells potions and
posts, there's something to all of this applying that equals prayer. I remember
seeing a girl scrolling down her feed on the subway while next to her a shawled
lady prayed the rosary and how they were the same motion. Also the woman in
Ex Machina walking away into nature that is her birthright. Is that what hap-
pens or did I wish it? A modernist and Romantic heritage peeks through like the
first flowers of spring…I'm feeling along with everything, and I have a spell-
book just like what I saw in *Teen Witch*. I hear "Violet" by Hole… Can you read
this book too and can we talk about it on a full moon?
—Ana Božičević

READY
FOR
THE
WORLD

Becca Klaver

Black
Lawrence
Press

www.blacklawrence.com

Executive Editor: Diane Goettel
Cover Design: Zoe Norvell
Book Design: Amy Freels

Copyright © Becca Klaver 2020
ISBN: 978-1-62557-810-5

All rights reserved. Except for brief quotations in critical articles or reviews,
no part of this book may be reproduced in any manner without prior written
permission from the publisher: editors@blacklawrencepress.com

Published 2020 by Black Lawrence Press.
Printed in the United States.

for my girls

...many feminists...have cast the project of "becoming woman" as one in which the woman can only be complicit in a patriarchal order...

—J. Halberstam, *The Queer Art of Failure*

                oh each poet's a
beautiful human girl who must die.

—Alice Notley, "World's Bliss"

Contents

The Woods

I never go to the woods anymore
But when I go to the woods
I remember
How to burn things at water's edge
If I never go to the woods again
I'll live to die another
Die to live another day
In the woods I just fan myself out among the mosses
Place my laptop gingerly on a stump
Set a timer for the webcam
Hug a tree and
A squirrel comes to visit me
Could I ever really live and love in the woods
I muse
Grinding my cigarette beneath the bower
What is the sorrow sound of this wood
The creak or the crickets
In the woods I see my sisters
They are there and there and there
Walking in figure eights
With their hands full
I dance around them
Little pyro with a lust for making
Lugging logs to the fire

Manifesto of the Lyric Selfie

Our "I"s.
They are multiple.
We shuffle them
often as we like.
They can tag us.
We can untag ourselves.
We've got our
to-be-looked-at-ness
oh we have
got it.
We peer and cross.
Go lazy.
We're all girly.
We're pretty selfie.
We write our poems.
We write our manifestos.
While sitting in the photo booth.
While skipping down the street.
We think: If only my camera
could see me now.
There is a tranquil lyric
but we recollect emotion
with the speed of the feed.
We pose to show
the spontaneous overflow
of powerful feelings.
There are no more countrysides.
There are no more churchyards.
We smudge our vistas.

We flip the cam around.
What is burning in our little hearts?
Hashtags of interiority
licking like flames.
We had been reflective.
We have been reflected.

Spell for Good Weather

please don't rain
on our yonic
pyrotechnics

our wingèd
pink park
smoke

check the internet
against
the perfect skies

why do I have faith
in the lightness
of the drift

when the only thing
they've ever been
is changeable

Performativity

Stand on the widow's walk and watch the ships come in
Wait for you around every corner and boo-ya
Eat poison candy and barf a debutante barf
Wear my girl gang jacket in the style of Kris Kross
Dye dye dye my hair the color of my bleeding heart
Be the bedazzled bully on your block
The giffy troll in your comments feed
Put a hex on your IP address
Teach a class in black magic at a for-profit university
Play a teenage witch at an open mic back home
Play myself / with my real heart pinned on
Bad bad bad as I never was
And when the last sad song plays through my head
I'll be crying
I'm melting, I'm melting!
Swimming in a sea of so long
And you'll be feeling all my feelings

Anagnorisis

On the internet it is easy to love you

On the internet it is easy to love me

We let each other off the hook

We get to it when we can

We won't become known unless we tell our secrets, and we won't

Yet some days I feel recognized in the Greek sense

You know who I am—maybe even better

On the internet there is a scene

I am a player and am found out

Recognition not only of a person but of what a person stands for

What is the true nature of my self and my situation?

Fortune, love, or knowledge

After much pain, sometimes death or a wedding

Other times the stage just gets cleared

Sharing Settings

I began to worry that everything I wrote, I wrote because someone was listening. *Poetry is* over*heard. Eloquence supposes an audience.* The feed demands one. I tried to keep a diary again, to get that teenage feeling back, but I could only write about how the internet was the best and worst thing that ever happened to me. The internet stole my brain. Told me to share share share. But what if the only things worth sharing were the ones that languished for months, even years? I thought about Robert Duncan and shuddered. What about the need for feed my need to feed my need for feedback? I pressed the fucking lever. Over and over. Give me the pellet! Like like love! I tried to write into my dreams, to tell a truth I wouldn't dare post to the feed, but everyone was there, too—the ones from high school and from right across the street, faces in a book I turned in my sleep. If I didn't tag anyone, could I get away with it?

Spell for the Future

swipe a time machine

instaconjure a feeling

"look, I made my day
                    so old"

that it's already over

once you make it real—

polaroid-vinyl
                    nostalgia-
for-nostalgia-itself
                    real—

does the wish to be "in life"
reappear?

            want to move to

Detroit?   Milwaukee

Escondido

Like Machine

I am a like machine.
I do so like.
I press and click.
I am a like machine;
I know power makes me.
I am like a machine,
silent unless turned on.
I am the motherboard of artifice.
I am, like, too close to nature.

Witches of Space & Time

When Caolan commented to say she was at a rest stop in Darien

my first thought was *upon a peak in Darien*

and the second was *Historically—or was it geographically?—inaccurate*

but when I turned off the footnotes of my mind

I realized, *I, too, am near a peak in Darien,*
which is to say I am also in Connecticut, on a Greyhound bus heading back
    to New York,
and if we time this right, we can wave across I-95

For a while I stared at cars in a carsick way
                            latching my vision onto license plates

        Soon I began receiving updates via text message

We told each other what we knew of our coordinates in space and
    time—

milemarkers & marinas & Burger Kings & Chinese Buffets
        food gas lodging & scenic overlooks

Meanwhile
my feed fed me
Wangechi Mutu
National Coming Out Day
the zeitgeist of witches
and tips for making your skin look less tired

When Caolan texted *Hooot!*
I swiped over and typed *SUCCESS!*
on the thread we had going

I thought I had missed her

but when I asked if she had a busted front left fender
indeed she did

For all the looking down and typing

we miss each other

but I saw you on I-95
with my own two eyes

and told you the traffic
would clear up on your side

we used our eyes
and our tools

our tools and
our eyes

to find
that flash

overlap
of space and time

or what they call
coincidence

Spell for Actualizing Art

be a child
before the internet

make

need not be material

try beats on wall
conversation
arrangement
or

delay

Space or Time

When it was a wall, it was like writing on a whiteboard on a dorm room door, or the way Ashlee's parents let us paint the walls of her basement lair and even keep the turtle we caught up north, which we named Jack Deveraux. Those were the days of our lives.

Then they started calling it a timeline, but it was a lie: time was a math problem; time was a scheme and a scramble. The days all out of order. Whose highlights? A robot's theory of our desire.

I'm saying all this because I'm embarrassed—because we're not even that close but I really like your posts, I mean I "like" them a lot, so you're always at the top of my day.

They can't keep a tally of the inky bloom of my blushing. (Can they?)

Hey, you would love this.

Have we met?

I want to give you something real, but we live here now.

Spell for Lost Things

because you stole her phone

I lived in another decade
all afternoon

ring doorbells
walk long distances
discover bookshops

whoever you are, thief

you are scum
    &
stumble-upon
    &

changed
the time
in my day

Disney Princess Pageant

Saturday, November 19, 2011 at 9:30 PM - 4 AM EST
Brooklyn, NY

10 Went · 0 Interested

I'm Snow White.

We're telling the truth.... On the Internet.

This is the best party I've ever been to.

Fur. Fondue. Sylvia. Tangerines. High pitched cat's meow. Yeow. Lace. Vaporizing and a cheerleader almost saved by technicolor Indian chief.

This is my last birthday.

This is a slumber party. Without sleeping.

This party is a scam.

lets see if i can really post from my kindle. then all forms of internet will be represented

Girl plus

Is this party on google +

If he really likes you he's Facestalking you, so he knows where you are.

I'm going to need some more cheese.

Who's your rising princess?

Dildos!

Spoiler alert!

I wanted to have a lot of food in my mouth when I read this line.

This is very serious. It's a diptych.

"The Hills" is universal. Like Michael Jackson.

first ten bars of the original 90210 theme song, GO

still contend it sounds like "a little bit dangerous"

shocker fave 90210 character is andrea.

Saved by the Bell: The College Years. That shit was hot.

--- we are quiet because the reading is now taking place ---

Breaking Dawn was trash. I'll stick to the books.

so many fantasy references from supathroat

Wonderwall singalong!

I'm totally still partying with y'all post party. While flossing. Removing contacts. Looking for sleeping socks.

Were Pocahantas and Mulan princesses? This is a hot topic right now.

You girlz and guyz made my bday perfect. Thank you.

This virtual party is still raging! even in the spaces between physical parties, where the wind is kinda cold (important part of princess [hero[ine]'s] journey.)

last guest has now left kate's last birthday party, thank you for joining us for this meta-pageant, much love, night night! <3

Nice to Meet You

I am always waiting for you to do that thing
Do that thing to show you're one of my tribe
I am always waiting for you to do that thing
For you to do that thing to show you're one
Of my tribe I am always waiting for you to do
That thing do that thing to show you're one
Of my tribe I am always waiting for you to do
That thing do do do that thing to show you're
One of my tribe I am always waiting for you
To do that thing do that thing to show you're
One of my I am always waiting for you to do
That thing do do do that thing to show you're
One of my tribe I am always waiting for you

The Slumber Party

Kate was playing Molly
breaking up
   w/ her boyfriend
(who knows if he's real)
It made Lorraine cry
   4 real
& then Lara caught the sads
   They call this
   "flows of affect"
contagion
   where each girl's
tears are more viral than
  the last
(or they're plastic beads....)
  Your feelings got in my eye
  they're mine now
    & crusted

Spell for Going Out

On the street
you said you wanted
to put a hit on the moon

At the show
the tote read

CRIME ON THE MOON

We were cousins
or mom & kid
or separated at birth

Where are we?

"Near a cop shop & a
career professional school"

That girl could really shred

jagged little icicle stars

"the moon says no!"

YES

Spell for a Hangover

first   friendship

2   *water saltines ginger ale*
          eggs watermelon seltzer
          bagels bitters coconut water

3   life obligations
         pressure to "show up"

you didn't mean to steal it
say that

you poisoned yourself now
you puked yourself

sure I'll come over

spill my cures on the table

   'mancy that

Spell for a Winning Team

—It sank 103 years ago today.
—Ships can have sisters?

Something connects rounds two, four, and six.
Famous Scientists, Current Events, War.

—I'm so sick of ideas of history that take place on battlefields.
—I know. It should all be about the domestic social.

Houses feud in mid-fifteenth-century England.
Mary McCarthy, group of Vassar girls, '33.

—Shhhh.
—Try to write things down without saying them aloud.

I is an island

Five women who grew up in a cold northern place land on an island and drink rum punch in the sun. No one remembers or knows she remembers anything except the one who has brought them there, the one who lives on the island now, the one who remembers everything. They climb to the heights and walk with the monkeys and swim with the turtles and buy bracelets and bags on the side of the road. They drive until they get lost in a downpour. None of the streets have names. They follow his directions to turn left, find the cricket field, look for the sun, and turn toward it. In every direction they see the sea. They find their way back. They tell the stories of all the times they had been there and hear the stories of all the times they had not been there. They do not remember some of the times when they had been there, so it is all the same. It is now as if they had all been there every time. It is as if they were there now. *Memory is a sense of the other.* What would have become of them had they not remembered. There was a keeper, the one who brought them there. One speaks; one becomes a subject. The girls grew up in the north, landed on an island near the equator, drank punch, made new memories. Unforgettable for all or some.

Hooliganism Was the Charge

In a 1993 study published in *Ethology* journal, "Laughter Punctuates Speech: Linguistic, Social, and Gender Contexts of Laughter," Robert R. Provine finds that

> *females are the leading laughers. Future research should evaluate the extent to which the pattern of laughter described here is the consequence of a vocal display performed by subservient individuals in response to dominant group members. For example, do subservient males show a female-like laugh pattern in the presence of a domineering male or female boss?*

On a Social Anxiety Support message board, a user named WintersTale writes:

> *I went out to eat for dinner with my grandma and my mom, and of course the waiter sat us down right next to a table full of high school girls. Who were giggling. When I sat down, I heard "eww, that's disgusting", which I attributed to me (maybe it wasn't, but it seemed too coincidental), followed by tons of giggling. I switched seats, so at least I wasn't sitting directly in front of them, but I still felt them looking at me and giggling.*

person86 replies:

> *I always assume that groups of teenage girls who are looking in my direction and giggling are checkin' me out. Maybe I'm just a conceited b*stard, but it makes a tad more sense.*

Zephyr replies:

> *Yeah I wouldn't really take it personally. Ducks go quack. Cows go mooooo. Dogs go woof. Teenage girls giggle. Sheep go baaa. Pigs go oink. I think they teach these concepts in kindergarten. It's hard to get mad at things that can only do what they're built for.* *shrug*

In "Some Observations on Humor and Laughter in Young Adolescent Girls," published in the *Journal of Youth and Adolescence* in 1974, Rita Ransohoff writes:

> *The contagion effect of hysterical laughter was observed among the girls. Hysterical laughter itself seemed to serve a group function. It offered reassurance which said "You are not alone; I can hear you."*

She offers an example:

> *Connie and Sally faced each other. They laughed in paroxysms. They maintained eye contact and when one would stop the other would start, and then they would laugh again together.*

In "The Laugh of the Medusa," Hélène Cixous writes:

> *If she's a her-she, it's in order to smash everything, to shatter the framework of institutions, to blow up the law, to break up the 'truth' with laughter.*

I wrote:

> *But laughter in the face of the law is infuriating, unjustifiable, anarchic.*

Pussy Riot smirking and cackling in their wood-and-glass cage, blowing up the law.

Hooliganism was the charge. Laughing inside the wrong doors.

To blow off and up a world that was not made for them.

It goes loud and long. Starts in the belly and you cannot stop it.

I leave the room where the girls sit in a circle and I can't hear words, only giggling.

I think to myself: *Liberation of subjugated energies.*

I think: *Intimacy of intimacies.*

Spell we put each other under.

I return to the room and say: *This is my favorite place in the world.*

Jenny and me in the cafeteria. They'd ask, *Are you mocking me?* They'd say *laughing at.* We were.

We were finding out that the world was not for us. We couldn't *laugh with.* We were taking what we could.

I laugh and laugh and laugh and keep laughing and I know it's magic because it gets the right people mad, the ones who want me to shut up, the ones who say silly girl, valley girl, too-much spilling-over seeping-out girl.

Me and my sisters grabbing each other's forearms in paroxysms, crying-laughing, knowing-we-were-interrupting-Mass-laughing, wanting to, wanting to see what would happen: *to shatter the framework of institutions…*

I googled "giggling girls," and the top two results were both titled "Giggling Girls and Bloody Violence."

Riotous release of the rrrrrrrrrrrepressed

—Oh my god I'm *dying*
—Oh my god *please stop*

Laughter as the last power
once you've traded in the rest.

The world had no use for them.
You just kept laughing it off.
No big deal.

The charge was hooliganism.
A refusal punishable by law.
The patriarch was offended personally.
Big guy in the sky can tell it's *laugh at*.

Look repentant or laugh
in the face of the law.

Can you hear my voice?

Valley-plaintive.

Totally.

It was a tear in
it was a ripple in
it was a giggle in space-time

the way we stayed girls
all those years

a style of being
that said

don't die too soon

just try to stay amused

—Oh my god I'm *dying*, oh my god *please stop*

I stopped practicing magic

      except on the internet   except in poems

        except when I laughed in your face at the very wrongest moment

We hold each other's gazes   and the first one to laugh wins

Like all rituals   it gets you ready for the world

Uptalk

It's like a phobia of life in general?

I promised not to do it again?

I paid you already?

I know you care, but it's not enough?

I think you need to bring your voice down?

I ate the rest of it?

I'm 100% positive I left it right here?

I didn't think that applied to me?

I kinda miss it?

I told them I'd be there every Thursday?

I keep getting what I want?

I sorta wanna flake on my own party?

It's, like, a tendency toward self-destruction?

I was thinking of the greater good?

I'm Crazy

I believe in
an outside

to the patriarchy
called

my
vanity

Becoming-Girly

First they stole yours

then you went a-roaming

on the body without organs

and you belong nowhere

not to *age group, sex, order, or kingdom*

but we become you

we become you

getting girly is getting down

while you, fugitive,

introduce one territory

to another

she did too many things,

crossed too many spaces....

why're you so slow

girl you're late you've been

all over the place

while we sit

here waiting thinking

girl

you're all speed and slowness

no not even that

relations of speed and slowness

modal

relative

so there you go, girl

you know

we better watch out

now you're speedy

we're slow

Style Power

He says you become
a body when tools of the law
exert themselves over the flesh
that render the idea 'your body'

She sings
never give away
never give away
your body

& build your style of being
out of thrifted jean jackets &
duct tape arrows pointing up
busk & bask in the underbelly

never give away
but gild with ornament
gleaming in the face
of the law

Vanity Mirror

Just because you're here   doesn't mean you've passed through

the glass is water   there's a timelag   on the other side

potions of belief   sandpaper for your doubts

I traded it in   & now they're telling me

to try   to get it back   to get it back different

as if a fire by the lake with a circle of girls smoking leaves

from the forest floor   were possible now

In the night stories too   I am alone   strange people land water

a felled tree   you either walk across or you don't

I have to go on finding things where I don't know to look

it hurts

I prefer browsing   clicking   piddling

twenty-seven   it's time to choose

tighten all my bows   take big gulps of air

take stock take stock take stock   fingertips to the glass

before diving into the pool   where we listen watch wait

speak underwater   in the light of practice

Entrance to the Tunnel Marked 'Lakefront'

Museums against the water.
Cameras come out in hordes.
The relief of many lenses.
Inner organs mirror the landscape.
You know what's on the other side:
a turning back, the girl. You even know
the troll, one good eye on the pan pipes.
Further back, at the roots of words,
doric time, ionic time, the bottom
of the sky a moment after the set,
bruised and maybe gone forever.

Diurnal

the life in a day
    nested again

        circuit's line
           in flattened space

            full spin thru
            thousands of twilights

          when I am mournful
       but round and full

    quick to turn on heel
to see what follows

Don't Look Back

stick to the muddy skirt
of your backglance

though the moral
shakes your shoulders
with curling yellow nails

though the street teaches
where to hover your gaze

   (little pocket of air
   your nose follows)

stray
& you are salt
or hag
or your predictions

"bigger guns
       to come!"

draw scoffs

&/or another piss-poor
mytho-way of saying

where a girl goes
when she doesn't go woman

Sleight of Hand

Who knows
　　where the time goes
months to years
　　like scarves to doves

The dish ran away with the spoon
　　And be you blithe and bonny
Your coachman awaiteth
　　in a punchbuggy orange no returns

"We was girls together"
　　The cobweb breaks and blows away
but the hourglass
　　keeps drizzling

"Stay with the young girls and the old"
　　as far off they line up
ringing the doorbell
　　ready for the game

Spell for Rebirth

Two masses a week minimum
(one in school, one on Sundays)

until, child of lawyers,
I argued my way out

using logic, the magic
of laying out one's case

Later, as in
a fairytale bargain

I was allowed to roam
only inside reason's rule.

Then I knew I could get it back.

Not the return the elders imagined—

doesn't take me to church or castle
or Vale of Enna

but drops me far afield—

> *take five balls of yarn*
> *state an ingrained belief*
> *as you unwind*
> *make a web*
> *describe the entanglements*
> *cut what you need to*
> *elsewhere make knots & bows*

I kept ritual and incense

       syncretic   heretic

  "How did you get born again?"

The ones who hunted witches

   taught me to believe in miracles

Clear It Out

Dear Mom the things in my girlroom are not flotsam or jetsam but lagan: I have buoyed them there to be tugged up later.

Don't expect me to yarn-tie cartons to my legs and drag them down the highway; don't call me baglady bride of the continental aisle.

I leave them afloat, recoverable. I leave a trail send up a flare for the stars to witness in ten thousand years.

You asked if it was sentiment. No.

I mumbled something about time and its lack. Untrue.

It was a queasiness in the hall of mirrors. How can I look myselves in the eye without bloodying my palm?

If you wanna talk, you can find me where I meant to go a decade ago. The other coast.

I won't cry this time, but I'll pack gauze and tape.

And you, Mom, from what dream will you wake up? What will you have forgotten to miss?

Mermaid Tale

I had her legs

I stole her tradeoff

The sea knew more

The land loved me better

Reproductive Logic

I think my parents are in town, but I haven't heard anything yet. It is a giant city with a drooling maw. They're probably smiling and squeaking toys in a faraway borough. I start to suspect that I am not really part of the family, that the way you get invited to the family is by having a family of your own. I am in my pajamas with the cats. By the logic of reproduction, I am the cat's pajamas. It's true what they say—you can defer being a real person indefinitely. Every day, I type my sentences and take my walks and my simple meals with wine. Every night I assert my rights. The women who tell me their husbands are their kids. The women up all night, strolling the day away. A while back I received an itinerary. Today it's easy to feel assured the flight has landed. By the logic of families, I am the errant son. As the princess in the tower, I am obliged to wave a pink scarf occasionally, and with desperation. Last night, I pulled the death card for future and shuddered as I thought, It's coming for us all; have your babies. I'll raise this solitude like a foundling. By tonight, someone will have accused me of not showing up.

Spell for Paying Attention

far-off song coming
through the mic
behind her words

frees? fuses? flees?

turn off
tune out

sometimes I just go somewhere else

"what are you staring at?"

the sounds the throat makes
close to the brain

Spell for Shadow Work

I haven't brought out

my hexes yet

but now it's late

at the party

and smoke's

filling the room

Kitty's First Lunar Eclipse

Jumps as if chased
or wounded

batting jacks
in the dark

The moon went out
rotting, rotating

marble-hard
between the molars

We were sooted with sleep
We were dead-black with Christmas

We saw no stars but those cracking
against our chests

diving bells
ringing

Spell for Feeling Different

He'd say he wanted to feel different
But all she knew were children's games

Medicine in the forest
Cash crops & government pills

Herbs out in the desert
Numb or cure those ills

She'd try to help him feel different
He'd say he always felt the same

The priestess rose up from the water
Then sank down with the rains

Legal and lethal, the salty pressure
cutting through her veins

He'd say, I just want to feel different
She'd say she always felt the same

Spell for Intuition

once your body knows
what hasn't climbed all the way up—

legs of lead
gut of knives

solar plexus bomb
of woven wires

you put your arm up:

north, south, east, west

earth, air, fire, water

past, present, future

flattened

what you need to know

however not-at-home

keeps you walking

with the wind you hailed

Astro-Luv (Harmony of the Worlds)

As for whether
I'm an astronomer
or astrologer

I come from a time
when there was
no difference

and I've been around
long enough
to see

all the ways
to kill witches
including

rock-drowning, stake-burning
clean beheading, botched
beheading

and most ruthless of all
the smothering
of memory

so the things
our bones know
get shut up for good

planets falling
toward the sun

girl, you better
run run run

★

That's why
groups of girls
are dangerous

are always
covenish
because we say

"neither astronomy
nor astrology"
(curtsy)

"dedicated to astro-
luv in all its forms"
(pinkies out)

"eye of newt
and scroll of blog"
(stir)

because
in a circle
of belief

we come to find
what we already
know

*planets falling
toward the sun*

*girl, you better
run run run*

As for whether
I read the stars
to divine the future

or improve
modern civilization
just

lie next to me
for a while
and stare at the sky

I deleted my
stargazer app
after the position

of the sun
under my feet
through the hill

and the earth's core
gave me such
a scare

I preferred
my human tools
after all

planets falling
toward the sun

girl, you better
run run run

A certain degree
of superstition
I've always allowed—

wishing, clenching,
blinking, flipping
a light switch—

what I don't know
minus
what I believe

Spring and sunrise
returning again
and again

though
we're the ones
spinning

What's superstition
but faith
but a tango

with late winter
ending in a
bloody kiss

planets falling
toward the sun

girl, you better
run run run

★

If we could
believe
in a world like this

might as well
wish
for another

The old rituals
ripped
from their targets

so we fill the gap
with names
of disorders

As for whether
I'm an astronomer
or astrologer

don't try and tell me
about stars
as they really are

I've felt my dwarfed will
poised where
the void doesn't end

planets falling
toward the sun

girl, you better
run run run

As for whether—
I have always
known

how to make
one thing
stand for another

I've lain on my back
and used
my hands and eyes

to trace pictures
in the sky—
to guess

at the future
like any other
instrument

inside some other
dimension's
black hole

That such a dark life
could be ruled by
such bright stars

Chorus 3x

Kitty's Second Lunar Eclipse

You lie
down in wait

for the potato
to bake.

I dream
of a clowder

eating
their own.

She's found
new

places
to hide.

We can't just
pretend

everything's
normal.

The shadow
coning

into the moon
is us.

Spell for Protection

I walk alone on dark streets

I walk alone on dark streets all the time

am I not supposed to do that

anymore   yet   again   still

.

.

.

feels like winter tonight

from my corner window I can see the armory turrets

it's a men's shelter

my sister says

for murderers and rapists without families

who got out

but they're still in

she runs a clinic on the other side of town

.

.

.

what are you afraid of and

what does that say about you

say about yourself:

I'm not afraid

I'm not afraid

I'm not afraid

.

.

.

all the men surprised to learn

how it is

what street do they live on

not ours

the night cracks in half

you float on your piece

I on mine

to take whichever way home

.

.

.

for protection I was given

many varieties of stone

so far I have not gotten

much more hurt

Spell for a Headache

warm saltwater cut

with baking powder

poured through

your face holes

or little blue pill

or forward fold

or water then wine

or sometimes

you spend all day learning

all over again

the ritual is just

sit

wait

let the weather roll through

Kitty's Third Lunar Eclipse

the clawbone's
  connected

to the
  eyebone

you didn't greet me
  in bed

or beg for food
  in the kitchen

you're standing
  on the table

staring out the window
  staring back at me

you can't say
  what you saw

did you see
  did you see

the rotted tooth
  of god

with night
  vision at dawn

I've got my bloody
   eye on you

here comes the sun
   little one

ever slicing
   slivers for the pile

Spell for the City

very spring day
coming down

sense of cycles
& returns

seventeen
on the coast

went out wishing
then kept

my promise
to myself

in spite of all
it's cost me

blossom-clouds
blow down

shadowy village blocks
and disperse

even the lost
impossibles

join me
here

Spell for the Health of a Heroine

The myths are gone   and in their place

                    a pink geometry

The only way out is in

                    rule of breath
                    & water
                    & songs that burn
                    beside you
                    till one day
                    you get up
                    from that rock

dry six tomatoes in the sun
  add a pinch of every condiment in the fridge door that hasn't turned
  do a headstand or imagining is just as good
    refresh your feed six times then chant the first six words of the top post six times

                    find a star
                    lacking that
                    a satellite
                    lacking that
                    close your eyes

anything can become a myth   anyone can become a heroine

        "To the health of those who've healed us"

Wish Piece

There might be room for wishes.

There might be, in this room, a place for wishes.

You might find on these walls the scum of wishes.

You might find the snail-slime of wishes.

You might have cleared out all your stuff, but you can't remove the wishes.

Not even with a magic eraser.

Not even with your tongue.

Not even with more wishes.

There might be room for wishes.

Wishes might be okay to leave behind.

You might say, I loved this place, and will to it my wishes.

A bequest of wishes.

You might say, Good riddance, I hope I never step foot in this place again.

A wish, of course.

For richer or for poorer, wishes.

In sickness many wishes and in health, fewer wishes, but a salutary wish good as any tonic.

The good fortune of rising bubbles.

Why not get up and make a wish?

Who knows who will catch it?

There are wishcatchers among us.

You will spot their feathers and beads. They will hang willingly.

Who among us is a wishcatcher?

For some, no wishes.

But wishing is not a luxury.

A wish is a want is an ache.

A wanton ache.

There might be room for wishes.

In this room, a place for wishes.

There might be, for use in the deployment of wishes, some pencils and some markers, in many colors.

Wishes could leave their snail trails on the walls.

You could write a wish or draw a wish or let a wish choose its own form.

Some will have a wish pushing against the inside of the chest. I wish those would get up and take a marker or a pencil in one of many colors and scrawl their wishes on the wall.

Some will have a wish that is a secret wish, but also, does anyone know your handwriting? Anymore? And could you write with your other hand?

It might be worth it for a wish.

Shaky wishes welcome. Risk of exposure welcome.

There might be room for wishes.

Some will say, Nothing urgent, pretty okay, pretty good, pretty satisfied, but why not wish during this, your one life on earth, perhaps?

To wish to return to earth better able to wish is a possible wish.

Wishing for more wishes welcome.

All wishes welcome.

There are wishcatchers among us.

Let us hope they use their powers for good.

You'll say I can't grant wishes, but I'll say you can, too.

Find a wish you can grant and circle it.

Make a wish that the wisher beside you can grant.

Wish that wishes be granted.

Wish for more wishes.

We can have no more wishes, wrote Gertrude Stein to a photographer, *because anything we wish is as we wish and though we are wishes always Gertrude Stein. P.S. And yet we wish well of course we wish.*

Of course we wish—we are wishes. This is to say desire exists as much as anything, and we are it.

Find a wish you can grant and circle it and write your phone number next to it.

If you'd like to see your wish granted, take that number and send a message up to the sky and it will bounce back to earth and perhaps be granted standard rates apply.

If you can't find a wish you can make, find a wish you can grant.

This is a reverse exorcism.

We are making wishes material, but wishes need not be visible.

You can just sit still, wishing.

So there is always room for wishes.

Many things are already gone from this home, many tables and lamps and sponges and tampons.

But there's always room for wishes.

How many wishes dropped into the blender how many wishes hanging over the toilet how many wishes climb the spiral stair.

There's always room for wishes, even if fishes were wishes.

There might be, in this room, a place for the scum the trail the echo the trace the fodder the kindling the color of wishes.

They will say that you are not free to wish.

They will use dirty words like *agency* and *ideology*.

They will tell you that you have been alienated from your wishes, that your wishes have been programmed out of you, that you have been hailed as wishless, the forces they had ranged against you, the forces you had ranged within you, but I am here to tell you it doesn't hurt to make one small wish and if you make a small wish the chances that it will be a bad wish seem even smaller.

A wish is large is never small.

They will tell you you can have no more wishes.

And yet we wish well of course we wish.

Spell for Ordinary Benediction

have fun

good luck

safe travels

be well

take care

bless you

feel better

no worries

good night

Spell for Heart Opening

In all the yoga classes
they were showing poses for heart opening

In all my dreams
post-fireworks smoke hung in the air

In the backseat of the convertible
I took off my rose-tinted sunglasses

only to see the world was still pink
underneath

><

shiver   sweat   sneeze
breathe   beat   love

things that go on without us

the body remakes itself

grows / up

><

How are we supposed to open our hearts
if spring keeps getting snatched away

How am I supposed to open my heart
when it folded down to its silty floor

><

sunglasses
pyrotechnics
camatkarasana

><

for the first time
I don't want spring to come

ice floes moan
"open your heart"

it's ridiculous to need
to be reminded

though anything
can close it off

even a wild devotion

><

roll your shoulders back
look out the window of a lamplit house
see your reflection stamped upon the sky

Spell for Knowing What You Want

Cast the dice repeatedly until you know the difference between numbers. Each one should give you a different feeling, like three is bland, six is a homecoming, two is the face of the thing in the closet. Then try dropping some marbles and letting them roll around until you learn something new yet obvious about where you are. The place has been slanted this whole time. You've been overcompensating. Try leaning differently. Lastly, get a mirror and tilt it until you can see the room to step into.

The Female Gaze

Obsessive & sensual

    but I don't want to say

closer to the body

      as if women

scuffed hooves

  in a pen

     together

    or as if the brain

weren't a moldable

  lump

Where she saw blue

   everywhere

     I imagine

  a lighthouse

scanning

ghost ships

where others see none

but as if

the fingertips were

(tics in the dark)

doing the looking

Spell for the Solstice

standing still with the sun
because why go on

side-eyeing the moon
who still sees me

I can't believe it's this day again
and I'm just me coming 'round

if this light is the most
I may ever feel

maybe I shouldn't hold
onto darkness

the need to edge out the sky—
what is it?

to smuggle air
like soil

★

by now you might think
you have all the light

in the world
and you do

the next feat is to stay graceful
while you give it up

★

on the darkest day
you'll know

you'll lose so much more
than you ever imagined

★

daylight soaking surfaces

nightlight smoothing sheets

★

for sun temple
use body

for moon shrine
use eyes

now rest
in your waterbed
deep in the bower

Spell for Dispelling Power

rattling windows in a Chelsea studio

    Katybird warbles

« There was a woman from Seattle who
    totally channeled her shit

  The old man was killed by a knife »

    ghosts on the first floor

« I wouldn't want anything bigger
    It's a really old house »

The predecessor of the guru of the
American hero still hangs around

Tarot de Marseille François Chosson 1736

    tell a story about three things hanging on your wall
    pull three cards
    then set your intention

Lee Ann goes to get the Blake deck

    « You're worrying about nothing »

Women of Poetry, Child of Music, XVIII Moon

« You have the complete world in front of you »

Journey from hiding to hosting to seeing

« And you're brave »

What did I take that needs replacing

« But you have doubt »

What powers did I have to give up

« Are you a scryer »

The world has changed a lot, actually

welcome
cycles and returns

and beware

« The region that my name's from means
God's children »

The Hierophant

What do you worship   who do you believe

    how do you find out   without any

altars   gestures   big guy in the sky

    no nuzzling   cape folds

breathing into   the quiver

    under your ribs   that says   *No one*

what you adore   cracks spindly limbs

    through its pedestal   and seems to rule

all the way   to the vanishing point

    But you can get up   turn away

follow the grey brick wall   onto the scroll

    project   the light of the mind

lodge an intention   in the body

a kind of strategic essentialism   at the altars

    of power   where your knees are sore

and the guides   are gone   still

    there are many   ways of knowing

The Hierophant!   shows you what

    you don't believe   *(little skeptic turns on heel)*

    it's hard to imagine   any other life

when you've only got   your one face

    (turn around)   *(turn around)*   *(turn around)*

Spell for More Spells

may be granted

in some weathers

depending on

the quality of light

the stage of grief

the medium of magic

Acknowledgments & Notes

Thank you to the editors of the following publications, where versions of poems and performance scripts included in this book originally appeared: the Academy of American Poets' Poem-A-Day series, Columbia College Chicago's Library-As-Incubator Project for *Grimm's Fairy Tales, Columbia Poetry Review, Denver Quarterly, Fanzine, GlitterMOB, Grimoire, The Iowa Review* blog, *Jellyfish Magazine, LEVELER, Powder Keg, Shock of the Femme, the tiny,* and *What Fresh Witch Is This?*

"Astro-Luv (Harmony of the Worlds)" was written for a *Powder Keg* special issue responding to Carl Sagan; the poem title refers to a *Cosmos* episode title and to a recurring segment on The Real Housewives of Bohemia podcast. "The Hierophant" was written for Jennifer Tamayo's Futurepoem tarot deck. "Wish Piece" was performed at Mustard Beak's Tower of Terror at 1670 Gates Avenue in Queens on August 25, 2012, and is for Niina Pollari and Yoko Ono. "Hooliganism Was the Charge" was presented at "The Slumber Party," a group performance at the &Now Festival in Boulder, CO, on September 27, 2013, which also featured Marisa Crawford, Kate Durbin, Lara Glenum, Tim Jones-Yelvington, and Danielle Pafunda. The poem "The Slumber Party" refers to the same performance.

Line of "World's Bliss" from *Grave of Light* © 2006 by Alice Notley. Published by Wesleyan University Press and reprinted with permission. In "Hooliganism Was the Charge," the quotation from Robert Provine is reprinted by permission of the author, and the Rita Ransohoff quotation is reprinted by permission from Springer Nature Customer Service Centre GmbH: *Journal of Youth and Adolescence,* "Some Observations on Humor and Laughter in Young Adolescent Girls," © 1974.

"Manifesto of the Lyric Selfie" borrows language from Wordsworth's *Preface to Lyrical Ballads*. "Witches of Space and Time" quotes Keats's "On First Looking into Chapman's Homer." "Sharing Settings" borrows language from "What Is Poetry?" by John Stuart Mill. "Sleight of Hand" quotes Toni Morrison's *Sula* and Catherine Wagner's "Stay with the Young Girls and the Old" from *Nervous Device*. "Memory is a sense of the other" in "I is an island" comes from Michel de Certeau's *Arts de Faire*. "Becoming-Girly" riffs on Deleuze and Guattari's idea of "becoming-girl" and Halberstam's idea of "becoming woman" under patriarchy quoted in the epigraph. "Style Power" quotes Cat Power's song "Nothin' But Time" from the album *Sun*. "Disney Princess Pageant" lifts words from the mouths and devices of Hanna Andrews, Kate Durbin, Ben Fama, Olivia Harris, Paul Hughes, Lily Ladewig, Caolan Madden, and Christie Ann Reynolds. The "fireworks" and "pyrotechnics" in multiple poems refer to Judy Chicago's "A Butterfly for Brooklyn," presented in Prospect Park on April 26, 2014.

Thanks to everyone who provided language and inspiration for the spells, especially Lauren Besser, Katy Bohinc, Lee Ann Brown, Marisa Crawford, Cassandra Gillig, Krystal Languell, Joni Mitchell, Morgan Parker, Jennifer Tamayo, Sarah Torinus, and Stephanie Young.

Thanks to Marisa Crawford, Brandi Homan, MC Hyland, Caolan Madden, and Larissa Szporluk for providing feedback on early drafts of this book, and to the women of (G)IRL and Eric Komosa for offering thoughts on individual poems.

Thank you, Jessie, Annie, and Fro, for our queendom in the woods. Thanks to Heather, Jenny, Kate, Molly, Tanja, Tara, and the rest of our teenage coven. Thanks to Lauren for the reinitiation rites in the form of friendship-is-magic podcasting in the real world with cars and houses and time; thanks also to our lawyers, Austin King and Shawn Sebastian. Thank you, Arielle Greenberg, for our many conversations about girlhood and poetry, and thank you, David Trinidad, for bringing the occult into the classroom at 33 E. Congress. I'm grateful to everyone who attended the Stardust Sessions to explore esoteric and literary practices at 19 Brevoort Place, the apartment where many of these poems were conjured or co-created. Thanks to Mimi Winick and Laura Moran for the manna from heaven and other offerings. My friends have taken me from scarcity to abundance many times over.

Last but not least, thank you to Diane Goettel and the Black Lawrence Press open reading period readers for believing in this book.

Becca Klaver is a writer, teacher, editor, scholar, and literary collaboration conjurer. She is the author of several chapbooks and of the poetry collections *LA Liminal* (Kore Press), *Empire Wasted* (Bloof Books), and *Ready for the World* (Black Lawrence Press). A founding editor of the feminist poetry press Switchback Books, she is currently coediting, with Arielle Greenberg, the anthology *Electric Gurlesque* (Saturnalia Books). Becca holds degrees from the University of Southern California (BA), Columbia College Chicago (MFA), and Rutgers University (PhD), and is the Robert P. Dana Director of the Center for the Literary Arts at Cornell College. Born and raised in Milwaukee, she lives in Iowa City.